Christian Crafts from Nature's Gifts

by Anita Reith Stohs

illustrated by Becky Radtke

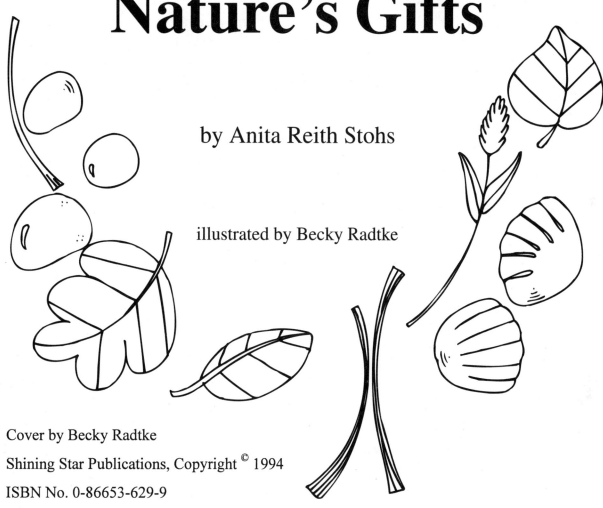

Cover by Becky Radtke

Shining Star Publications, Copyright © 1994

ISBN No. 0-86653-629-9

Standardized Subject Code TA ac

Printing No. 9876543

Shining Star Publications
A Division of Frank Schaffer Publications, Inc.
23740 Hawthorne Blvd.
Torrance, CA 90505

Unless otherwise indicated, the New International Version of the Bible was used in preparing the activities in this book.

Table of Contents

Shining Star Publications, Copyright © 1994

SS3847

Dedication

To Barbara Vaughan and the family of God at Hope:

May you grow in the love of God as you see more and more the marvelous handiwork of His created world. Psalm 19:1-4

To the Teacher/Parent

"The heavens declare the glory of God; the skies proclaim the work of his hands."

Psalm 19:1

This book contains a variety of craft projects made with objects gleaned from nature, from seeds to weeds. Children learn by doing, and these crafts were designed to help children better understand Bible lessons and celebrate God's handiwork. The finished crafts will serve as reminders of God's love and care. Keep in mind as you do these nature projects that it is the process, not the final product, that is most important. When you treasure your children's work, they will learn to treasure and value themselves.

These nature crafts will also help children appreciate the marvelous world God has created. Use the crafts to teach children to look closely at the treasures of nature God has given us. God told Adam to take care of the garden of Eden. As your students' eyes are opened to the wonders of God's creations, may they also become better caretakers of our planet.

Adapt individual activities to the ages of the children with whom you are working. You may need to adjust the materials used depending on the availability of certain objects in your part of the country. As children work on these crafts, lead them into discussions about the marvelous variety found in nature. Encourage them to follow God's creative example as they create their own unique crafts. Remind them that God did not make a carbon copy world. Doing crafts presents the perfect opportunity to help children develop and value their own unique artistic abilities and creativity. Each craft includes step-by-step directions, materials lists, and patterns. Children will make collages, mobiles, prints, weavings, dolls, puppets, toys, models, sculptures, plaques, ornaments and much more.

The Earth Shows His Handiwork

Layered-Sand Paperweight

Bible Story:
Creation. Genesis 1; Psalm 19:1

Materials:
Sand
Paper cups
Plastic spoons
Food coloring or tempera
Water
Glue
Construction paper
Marker
Scissors
Empty plastic jar

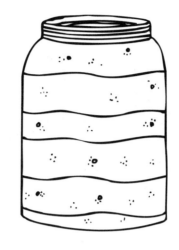 

Directions:
1. Place tempera or food coloring and a little water in different cups. Use earth tones such as brown, green, or yellow. Add sand to each cup. Mix. Leave some sand uncolored.
2. Carefully layer sand in the jar. Make sure the jar is completely full of sand.
3. Trace lid on paper. Write "The Earth Shows His Handiwork" on the circle. Cut out and glue to top of lid.
4. Glue lid to jar.
5. Place the jar where it will serve as a reminder to praise God for the wonderful land He made for His world.

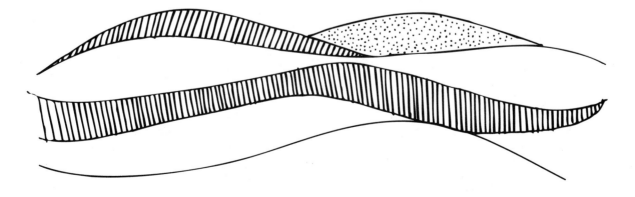

Sunshine and Starlight

Seed Collage

Bible Story:
Creation of the world. Genesis 1

Materials:
Cardboard
Dark blue construction paper
Glue
Seeds from a watermelon, cantaloupe,
    or pumpkin
Baking sheet
Pencil
Marker
Scissors
Cardboard tube
Masking tape

Directions:
1. Spread watermelon, cantaloupe, or pumpkin seeds on a baking sheet to dry.
2. Cut construction paper the same size as the cardboard.
3. Use a pencil to lightly outline a sun, moon, or star on the paper.
4. Glue on dried seeds, filling in the shapes you have drawn. Use different colors of seeds for outlining and details.
5. Write "Thank God for _____" on the picture, filling in the blank with appropriate words.
6. Tape a cardboard tube to the back of the picture so it will stand up. Let the collage remind you to thank God for His gift of sun, moon, and stars.

Other Ideas:
1. Combine several different shapes in the picture, such as the moon and several stars.
2. Omit construction paper and cover the entire cardboard with seeds set into a mixture of dough paste made by mixing 1 part salt, 1 part flour, and water.
3. As you work with the dried seeds, talk about how God's sun helps things grow.

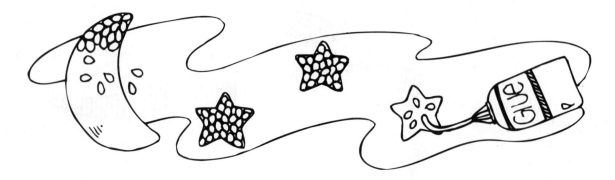

God's Colorful Creation

Waxed-Leaf Collage

Bible Story:
Creation of the world. Genesis 1

Materials:
Colorful fall leaves
Floor wax
Bowl
Thread
Coat hanger
Permanent marker
Scissors

Directions:
1. Collect fall leaves. Talk about how the leaves show some of the beautiful colors God put into His world.
2. Pour floor wax in the bottom of the bowl.
3. Cut a piece of thread and tie it to each leaf.
4. Dip each leaf into the floor wax. Hang it on the hanger to dry.
5. Use a permanent marker to write "God's Gift of Color" on one of the leaves.

Other Ideas:
1. Write a word on each leaf to express thanks to God.
2. Write a Bible passage emphasizing creation on a piece of construction paper and hang it from the coat hanger.
3. Use the collage for a lesson emphasizing God's creation of seasons.

Shining Star Publications, Copyright © 1994

SS3847

Feel God's World

Texture Collage

Bible Story:
Creation. Genesis 1

Materials:
Nature objects
Styrofoam™ tray
Glue
Permanent marker
Hole punch
Yarn
Scissors

Directions:
1. Collect nature objects illustrating a variety of textures: hard, soft, smooth, rough, silky, sticky, bumpy, etc.
2. Glue the different objects on a Styrofoam™ tray.
3. Write "Feel God's World" on the Styrofoam™.
4. Punch a hole at the top of the tray. To make a hanger, thread yarn through the hole and tie it in a knot. Hang the collage on the wall.
5. Thank God for the textures and for the gift of touch that enables us to feel them.

Other Ideas:
1. Cut a piece of burlap and glue it on the inside of the tray before attaching the objects.
2. Paint a piece of cardboard or a box lid to use instead of the Styrofoam™ tray.

SS3847

God's Tiny Creations

Dried-Flower Bouquet

Bible Story:
Creation. Genesis 1

Materials:
Dried weeds
Small, empty bottle
Ribbon
Round sticker
Fine-tipped markers
Paper bag

Directions:
1. Go on a nature hike and collect small, dry weeds. Place them in a paper bag. As you search, discuss the many wonderful little things God has placed in our world.
2. Write "God's Tiny Creations" on the sticker and stick it on the bottle.
3. Wrap a ribbon around the bottle and tie it in a bow.
4. Choose small, dry weeds to stick in the bottle.
5. Let the tiny weeds remind you of the importance of all God's creations, even tiny ones.

Other Ideas:
1. Before attaching the stickers, paint or spray the bottle with acrylic paint. (Adult supervision required.)
2. Instead of "God's Tiny Creations" write a Bible verse about creation on the sticker.
3. Use a plastic bottle instead of a glass one.

SS3847

Creatures That Creep and Fly

Walnut Shell Animals

Bible Story:
Creation. Genesis 1; Psalm 148

Materials:
English walnuts
Nutcracker
Construction paper
Glue
Markers
Box lid
Bark, rocks, and moss

Directions:
1. Carefully break English walnuts into halves and clean out the shells.
2. Talk about small animals God put on His planet. List animals that could be made from walnut shells. Examples: turtles and ladybugs.
3. Use construction paper cutouts to make the shells into animals. Add details with markers.
4. Glue bark, rocks, and moss on the box lid. Add animals.
5. Use a marker to write words from Psalm 148 around the outside of the box lid: "Small Creatures and Flying Birds … Praise the LORD!"

All God's Creatures

Potato Creations

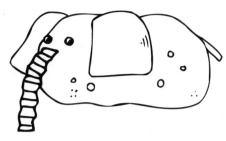

Bible Story:
Creation. Genesis 1

Materials:
Odd-shaped potatoes
Toothpicks or matchsticks (with burnt ends)
Garden materials, such as leaves or sticks
Pantry materials, such as cloves or raisins
Kitchen paper products, such as
    cupcake liners or waxed paper
Fabric scraps, such as cloth and yarn
Flour-and-water paste

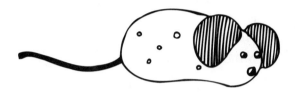

Directions:
1. Pick a potato and decide what animal in God's creation it most resembles.
2. Select materials that will help you turn your potato into that animal.
3. Poke in sticks and cloves, and glue on other materials with a paste of flour and water.
4. Thank God for the animal you made, as well as for the potato and other materials you used to make the animal.
5. After you have enjoyed your potato creation, clean it up so it can be turned into another gift of God's creation—food to eat.

Other Ideas:
1. Scrape a hole out of one side of a potato; then add matchstick legs and other details to turn it into an animal. Fill it with dirt and add grass seed. Set it in a sunny place and keep it moist. In a few days your animal creation will begin to grow hair. (Good for making a potato llama!)
2. Use food coloring to paint details on your potato animal.
3. Bake the potato. Use cheese and other toppings to turn it into an animal before eating it.
4. Make potato people to use as puppets.

SS3847

Safe with God

Shell Collage

Bible Story:

  The great flood. Genesis 6-8

Materials:

  Sheet of cork
  Scissors
  Gummed picture hanger
  Permanent markers
  Glue
  Small shells

Directions:

1. Duplicate and cut out the ark pattern on page 13. Trace the pattern on a sheet of cork and cut it out.
2. Use markers to draw the roof and bottom of the ark, as well as waves along the bottom of the ark.
3. Glue shells to the roof of the ark.
4. Glue shells to the ark deck. Use markers to add details to turn the shells into animals faces (or leave the shells unmarked for portholes).
5. Write "Safe with God" on the ark.
6. Attach the gummed hanger to the back of the ark. Let the ark be a reminder that you, like Noah and the animals, are safe with God.

Other Ideas:

1. Instead of using markers, glue yarn to the ark for details.
2. Cut out a dove shape and cover it with white shells.

Ark Pattern

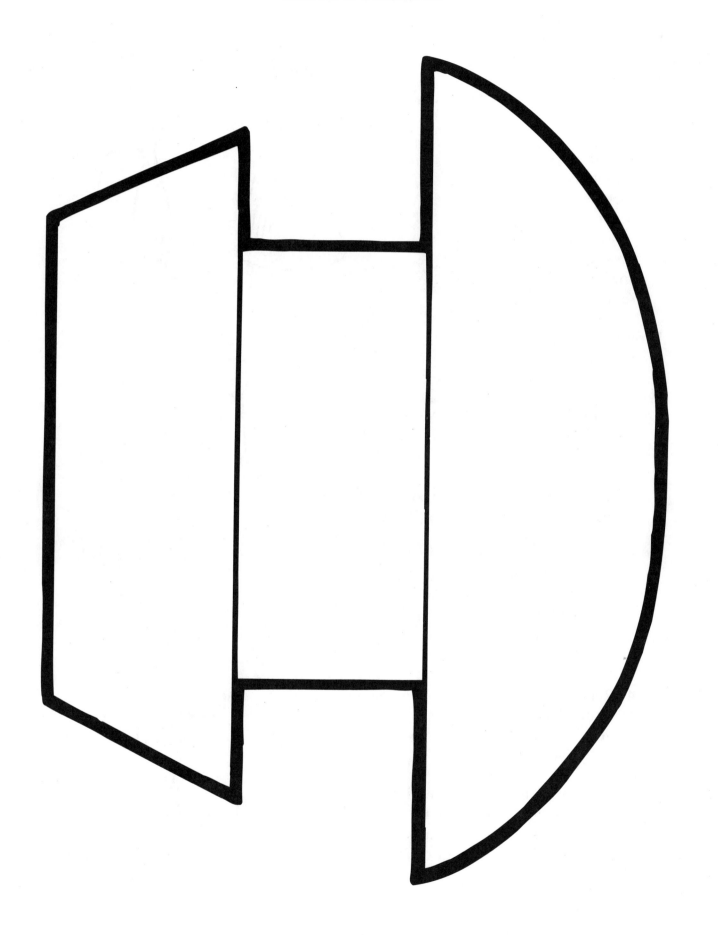

SS3847

To a New Land

Cornhusk People

Bible Story:
God calls Abraham to go to a new land.
Genesis 12:1-5

Materials:
Cornhusks
Chenille stems
String
Scissors
Markers
Bowl of water
Yarn

Directions:
To make Sarah:

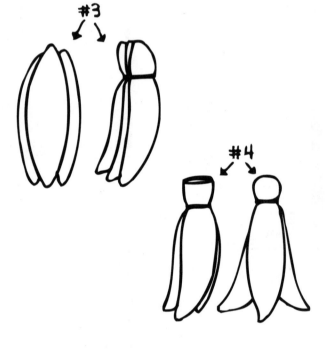

1. Dry husks by spreading them out on newspaper for several days until they are ivory colored. You will need the husks from three ears of corn to make each doll.

2. Soak the dried cornhusks about ten minutes in warm water until they are pliable.

3. To make the head and body, place two or three cornhusks on top of one another, fold them in half, and tie string about 1" from the top as shown.

4. Round the top of the head. Turn the figure upside down and peel the husk down. Pad the head with a rolled piece of cornhusk.

5. Form arms by rolling one or two cornhusks into a long cylinder. Trim it with scissors and make hands on each end by tying them off with string as shown.

6. Tie the figure at the waist with a piece of string.

#6 and #7

7. Fluff out the bottom of the husks and trim them for the skirt. Tie the arms down until they're dry.

8. Use a fine-tip marker to add facial details.

9. Glue on yarn for hair.

To make Abraham, add a yarn beard and add these steps:

#8 and #9

10. Slit the husks up to the waist, insert a chenille stem in each leg, and tie off the bottom of each leg with string. Fold up each chenille stem end to make a foot for each leg. Tie each foot.

11. Make a robe for Abraham by cutting two strips of cornhusk to place over each shoulder. Crisscross the strips over the front and back sides and tie them in place.

#10

12. Optional sleeves: Roll a cornhusk funnel for each arm, slip the narrow end over the arm, and tie it in place.

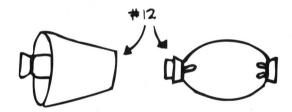

#12

13. Use your cornhusk people to tell the story of Abraham and Sarah's faithful journey to the land God had promised to them and their children.

Other Ideas:
1. Buy dried husks from a craft store.
2. Make cornhusk dolls for Mary and Joseph or other Bible characters.

#11

The Bush That Kept Burning

Stick Sculpture

Bible Story:
The burning bush. Exodus 3

Materials:
Oil-based clay
Twig
Red cellophane
Glue
Scissors
Plastic lid
Construction paper
Markers

Directions:

1. Cut construction paper to fit inside the plastic lid.
2. Write "I Am Who I Am" around the construction paper.
3. Glue the paper to the lid.
4. Place clay in the center of the lid. Stick the twig into the clay.
5. Cut strips of red cellophane (depending on the size of twig you are using). Crumple them around the branches of the twig to look like burning flames. Glue them on if necessary.
6. Moses had a job to do. Talk about what you can do for God and others.

Other Ideas:

1. Weave red tinsel and garland through the branches of the bush to represent fire.
2. Make a clay model of Moses to place next to the burning bush.
3. Dip red fall leaves in floor wax. Tie them to the twig.

Bible Characters

Plaster of Paris Eggs

Bible Story:
Bible Heroes.

Materials:
Raw egg
Straight pin
Toothpick
Plaster of Paris
Poster board
Markers
Tape
Glue
Yarn

Directions:
1. Thoroughly wash the egg. Use a straight pin to punch a hole in each end of the egg. Insert a toothpick in one hole to break up the yolk for easier blowing. Blow out the inside of the egg. Wash the egg and let it dry.
2. Tape one end of the egg to seal the hole.
3. Mix plaster of Paris according to the package directions. Pour it into the egg. Wipe off any excess plaster from the outside of the shell. Let the plaster harden for several hours.
4. Draw a face on the egg to represent a Bible character.
5. Add yarn hair.
6. Use the egg as a puppet to tell a Bible story.

Other Ideas:
1. Decorate the egg with water-soluble markers and cover with acrylic varnish.
2. Make an egg for each of the sons of Jacob or other Bible characters.
3. Make eggs with appropriate decorations for Easter or Christmas.
4. Paint the egg with watercolor, tempera, or acrylics.

Manna in the Wilderness

Woven Basket

Bible Story:
God provides for His people in the wilderness. Exodus 16:9-21

Material:
Thin cane or reeds
Bowl of water

Directions:
1. Soak cane in water about ten minutes before you weave.
2. Arrange eight long pieces, or ribs, in a cross.
3. Weave a long piece of cane in a circle in and out of the eight long ribs.
4. Add an uneven number of additional ribs to the weaving.
5. Weave in and out with new pieces of cane. Join pieces by weaving the new piece through five or six of the previous ribs.
6. When you have made the bottom of the basket as large as you wish, bend the ribs upward and then continue working.

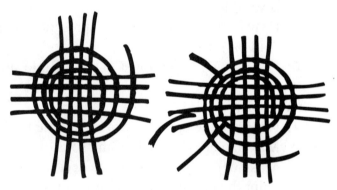

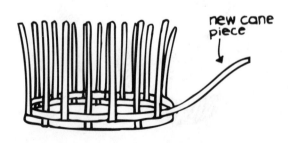

new cane piece

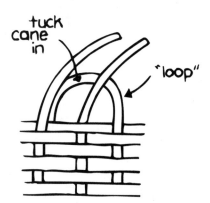

7. Cut all the ribs to the same length. Bend each rib past the next rib and tuck it in beside the second rib.

8. Leave a loop on top, or tuck in the rib for a smooth top edge.

9. Put snack crackers in your basket. Talk about how God gives you your food today.

Other Ideas:

1. Adapt the size of the baskets to the age of the children making them. Young children making small baskets may not need to add additional ribs.

2. Research to find other ways to weave baskets.

3. Find out ways baskets were used in Bible times; look in a Bible concordance to see how often baskets are mentioned in the Bible.

4. Paint the baskets when finished.

Land of Milk and Honey

Cornhusk Collage

Bible Story:

God shows Moses the Promised Land. Deuteronomy 34:1-4

Materials:

Cornhusks
Green fabric dye
Liquid dish detergent
Bowl
Poster board
Glue
Rubber gloves

Directions:

1. Buy cornhusks or make your own by spreading the husks of sweet or field corn on newspaper to dry for a few days.
2. To dye husks, place two teaspoons of fabric dye in a bowl and add very hot water. (An adult should do this.)
3. Wear rubber gloves when placing the husks in the dye for varied amounts of time. Dip them in and out for a light shade. Leave them in for an hour for a darker shade. Place the husks on newspaper to dry. Rinse them with cool, running water before using them.
4. Cut cornhusks into desired shapes and glue them on the poster board to make a picture of the beautiful land God showed Moses.

Other Ideas:

1. Use natural dyes found in the kitchen to color cornhusks: onion skins for rust, beet juice for red, grapes for purple, or turmeric for deep yellow.
2. Glue cornhusks to a box or box lid. Add dried flowers and weeds.
3. Make cornhusk collages for other Bible stories.

We Will Serve the Lord

Rock House

Bible Story:
   Joshua and his family serve the Lord.
   Joshua 24:14-15

Materials:
   Rock with flat side
   Fine-tip marker
   Acrylic paint
   Acrylic varnish (optional)
   Pointed round paintbrush

Directions:
   1. Place the rock on a flat surface in the best position for a house.
   2. Paint a roof, door, windows, and other features on the rock. If you wish, add family members.
   3. With a fine-tip marker write, "We Will Serve the Lord" on the rock.
   4. Paint the rock with acrylic varnish (optional).
   5. Set the rock in a spot where it will remind you and your family to choose, like Joshua, to serve the Lord.

Other Ideas:
   1. Use enamel paints for a glossy finish.
   2. Cover the rock with clear acrylic varnish before painting on the colors.
   3. Glue a felt base under the rock.
   4. Cover a brick with latex paint; then paint it with acrylic paint.
   5. Print your family name on the rock house.

Trust in God

Straw Cross

Bible Story:
Ruth and Naomi. Ruth 1:16-17; 2:12

Materials:
Pieces of straw
Glue
Poster board
Marker
Scissors

Directions:
1. Cut straw into equal lengths.
2. Write "Trust in God" in the center of the poster board.
3. Glue straws to the poster board, as shown.
4. Ruth went into the harvest fields to find food for Naomi and herself. There she met Boaz, who became her husband. Let your straw cross remind you, like Ruth, to trust in the Lord.

Other Ideas:
1. Glue the straw to a piece of cork or block of wood.
2. Bend the straws and weave them in the center to make a cross.
3. Glue other pieces of straw on top to make a decorative pattern.
4. Outline and fill in the shape of a bird with straw; then add the words of Boaz in Ruth 2:12.

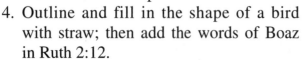
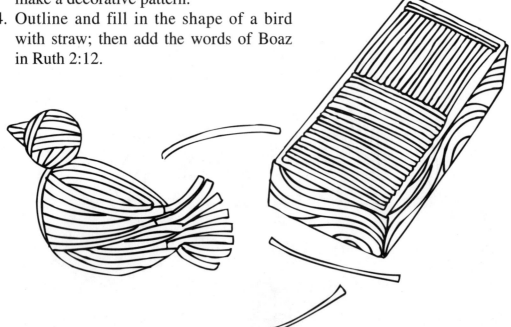

A Book for All Time

Cornhusk Scroll

Bible Story:
Josiah reads God's Word to his people. 2 Chronicles 34:29-33

Materials:
Sweet corn in husk
Newspaper
Bowl of water
Scissors
Marker
Cork sheet
Large paper clip
Toothpicks
Glue

Directions:
1. Just like Josiah of long ago, we need to read God's Word. Make a scroll to remind you to continue to grow in God's Word.
2. Husk the corn. Spread the green husks on newspaper. Let them stand several days until dry.
3. When you're ready to work, soak the husk in water for several minutes.
4. Cut the husk in the shape of a long rectangle.
5. Glue a toothpick to each end of the husk. Roll the husk around each toothpick, leaving about 2" in the center. Place a weight on the center and let the glued husk dry.
6. Cut a cork or paper circle larger than the cornhusk scroll.
7. Glue the husk scroll to the center of the cork circle.
8. Write the words, "Your word is a lamp to my feet and a light for my path" Psalm 119:105, around the cork circle.
9. Tape a large paper clip to the center top on the back of the cork. Hang the scroll in a place where you can see it each day and be reminded to look in the Bible for guidance.

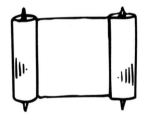
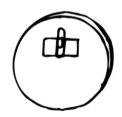

Other Ideas:
1. Write your favorite Bible verse inside the scroll.
2. Glue the scroll to a piece of bark or another kind of wood.

I Shall Not Be Moved

Pinecone Tree

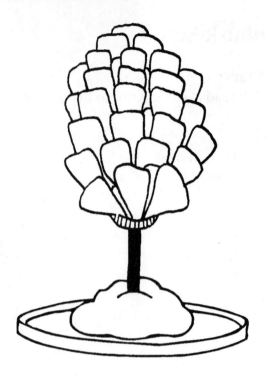

Bible Story:

The tree planted by the water. Psalm 1

Materials:

Pinecone (flat-bottom type)
Green acrylic paint
Brush
Stick
Modeling clay
Blue and green construction paper
Plastic lid
Markers
Scissors
Glue

Directions:

Before class the teacher should glue one end of a stick into the base of a pinecone. This will need to dry overnight so the children can follow these directions in class.

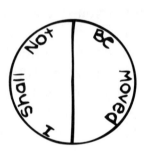

1. Paint the tips of the pinecone scales with green acrylic paint.
2. Make a ball of modeling clay. Press the other end of the stick in the clay.
3. Cut blue and green half circles to fit the plastic lid. Glue them into the lid.
4. Write "I Shall Not Be Moved" around the paper on the lid.
5. Stand up the tree and glue it to the center of the lid.
6. Let the tree remind you to stand firm in your faith in the Lord.

Other Ideas:

1. Write several verses from Psalm 1 on the lid.
2. Use your tree when you talk about other trees mentioned in the Bible.
3. Cut a cardboard circle; draw water and land on it with markers or crayons.

Praise the God of All Creation

Nature Brush

Bible Story:
The earth is full of the wonders of the Lord.
Psalm 104

Materials:
Large sheet of paper
Cups of tempera paint
Nature objects to use as brushes (twigs,
    evergreen branches, feathers, etc.)
Cup of water
Cassette tape of praise music
Tape player

Directions:
1. Make a printed-creation picture to praise God for His creation of our wonderful world.
2. Play praise music on the tape player.
3. While listening to the music, dip natural objects, such as twigs, branches, and feathers, in paint. Use large arm movements to paint your picture with "nature's paintbrushes."

Other Ideas:
1. Paint praise pictures for Christmas, Easter, or other holidays.
2. As a class, paint a wall mural using the natural objects as paintbrushes.

Saved from the Lions

Shell Puppets

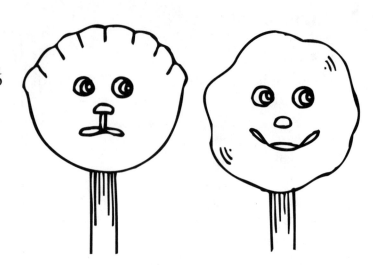

Bible Story:
Daniel in the lions' den. Daniel 6

Materials:
Two wooden spoons
Large cockleshell
Large mussel shell
Four small periwinkle shells
Several very small shells
Glue

Directions:
1. Use the mussel shell for Daniel and the cockleshell for the lion.
2. Glue periwinkle shells on the larger shells for eyes.
3. Glue very small shells on each large shell for a nose and mouth.
4. Glue each large shell on the wide end of a wooden spoon. Let them dry.
5. Use these to tell what happened when Daniel was thrown into the lions' den.

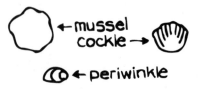

Other Ideas:
1. Make additional lion puppets.
2. Use large craft sticks instead of wooden spoons.
3. Substitute other kinds of shells to make the puppets.
4. Use a variety of shells to make other Bible character puppets.
5. Glue each shell face to a plastic lid and add a magnetic strip to the back for a refrigerator magnet.

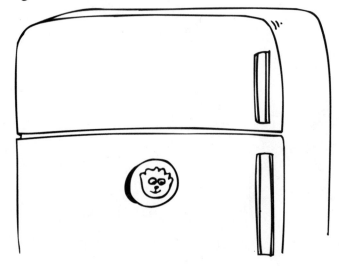

SS3847

Get Ready for Jesus

Pinecone Advent Wreath

Bible Story:

An angel appears to Zechariah. Luke 1:5-23

Materials:

Styrofoam™ paper plate
Permanent markers
Scissors
Small pinecones
Ribbon
Glue
Hole punch
Yarn

Directions:

1. Write "Get Ready for Jesus" in the center of the plate.
2. Glue pinecones around the plate rim.
3. Punch a hole at the top of the wreath. Make a yarn hanger by stringing a piece of yarn though the hole and securing it with a knot.
4. Tie a ribbon in a bow and glue it to the bottom of the wreath.
5. Put up your wreath as a reminder that it is Jesus' birthday you will be celebrating on Christmas Day.

Other Ideas:

1. Spray paint the wreath. (This should be done by an adult.)
2. Glue balls from a sweet gum tree or several different kinds of pinecones on the plate.
3. Cut out the center of the Styrofoam™ plate. Put the wreath on the table and set four candles in candleholders around it.
4. Wire the pinecones to a Styrofoam™ wreath or a coat hanger bent in a circle.
5. Make an Advent wreath by attaching a pinecone to the plate for each day in December until Christmas.

SS3847

Christmas Is Coming

Advent Garland

Bible Story:
   Gabriel appears to Mary. Luke 1:26-39

Materials:
   Pinecones
   Chenille stems
   Garland
   Glitter
   Glue
   Paper bag
   Religious Christmas stickers

Directions:
1. Mary had to prepare for Jesus' birth. You can prepare for His birthday, too, by adding pinecones to a garland each day before Christmas.
2. You will need a pinecone for each day of the four weeks before Christmas.
3. Add glitter to the pinecones by covering them with glue and shaking them one by one inside a paper bag of glitter. Then let them dry.
4. Stick a Christmas sticker on each pinecone.
5. Tie a chenille stem around the top of each pinecone.
6. Loop a string of garland on a tree or around the room.
7. Tie a pinecone on the garland each day of Advent.

Other Ideas:
   Alternate pinecones with paper stars. You may want to write words from favorite Christmas carols or Bible verses on the stars.

Sleep, Baby, Sleep

Nutshell Ornament

Bible Story:
Jesus' birth. Luke 2:1-7

Materials:
English walnut shell
Small peanut (in the shell)
Fine-tip marker
Fabric scraps
Scissors
Glue
Yarn

Directions:
1. Draw a face and hair on one end of the peanut.
2. Cut a strip of fabric. Glue it around the other end of the peanut.
3. Glue the peanut inside the walnut shell.
4. Cut two pieces of yarn. Glue them around the nutshell as shown. Knot the yarn at the top.
5. Place the nutshell ornament on your Christmas tree to remind you that Jesus, our Savior, first slept in a humble manger.

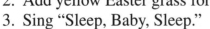
← yarn

Other Ideas:
1. Use a small plastic doll, available at craft stores, to represent Baby Jesus.
2. Add yellow Easter grass for straw.
3. Sing "Sleep, Baby, Sleep."

SS3847

Born in Bethlehem

Straw Drawing

Bible Story:
Jesus is born. Luke 2:1-7

Materials:
Straw
Craft glue
Blue poster board

Directions:
1. Using the sketch as a guide, outline the star, stable, and manger with straw.
2. Glue the straw in place.

Other Ideas:
1. Outline the star to illustrate the story of the wise men. Outline the word "Jesus" for the story about the naming of Jesus.
2. Substitute cardboard for poster board.
3. Cover the cardboard with burlap or wallpaper.
4. Use this straw drawing for other Bible stories, such as Creation, the great flood, Jacob's ladder, or Jesus' death and resurrection.

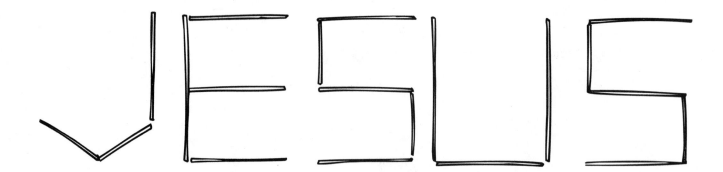

SS3847

Christ the Savior Is Born

Pinecone Manger Scene

Bible Story:
Jesus is born. Luke 2:1-20; Matthew 2:1-12

Materials:
Pinecones
Pine needles
Brown paper bag
Scissors
Markers or crayons
Glue
Cardboard box

Directions:

1. Cut pieces of a brown paper bag to cover the inside and outside of the cardboard box. Glue the pieces in place.

2. Turn the box sideways. Glue pine needles to the inside bottom. Glue some pine needles along the outside top.

3. Duplicate, color, and cut out the patterns on page 32.

4. Stand the pinecones upright. Glue each pattern to a pinecone.

5. Set the figures in and around the stable. Secure the star on top.

6. Use your pinecone figures to act out the Christmas story.

Other Ideas:

1. Tie strong thread to the tops of the pinecones and hang them on your Christmas tree.

2. Hang the figures from a dowel stick to make a mobile.

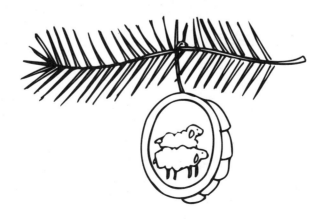

SS3847

Manger Scene Patterns

SS3847

Go, Tell It on the Mountain

Pinecone Bell

Bible Story:

Shepherds share the story of Jesus' birth. Luke 2:20

Materials:

Four pinecones
Yarn
Glitter
Glue
Four jingle bells
Paper bag
Scissors
Styrofoam™ egg carton
Permanent markers
Pen
Tape (optional)

Directions:

1. Cut a section of four egg cups from the egg carton.
2. Turn the egg cups upside down. Write "Jesus Christ Is Born" around the sides of the egg cups.
3. Use a pen to poke holes in the bottoms of the egg cups and in the middle of the section.
4. Dot glue on the pinecone. Shake it in a bag of glitter. Take it out and let it dry. Repeat with the other pinecones.

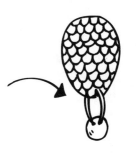

5. Thread 4" pieces of yarn through the tops of the jingle bells. Tie them to the tops of the pinecones.
6. Cut 4"-5" pieces of yarn. Tie each piece to the bottom of a pinecone.
7. Thread each piece of yarn through one of the holes in the bottom of an egg cup. Knot it on the other side (tape it in place, if necessary).

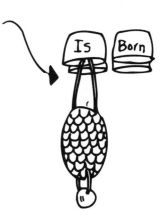

8. Cut a 10" piece of yarn. Thread one end though the center of the egg carton section. Knot it in place. Tie a loop in the other end for hanging.
9. Let the bells of your pinecone mobile remind you to join the shepherds in spreading the good news of your Savior's birth.

Follow That Star

Star Tree

Bible Story:
> Visit of the wise men. Matthew 2:1-12

Materials:
> Branch
> Empty bottle
> White paper
> Scissors
> Glitter (optional)
> Thread and needle

Directions:
1. Stick the branch into the empty bottle.
2. Make white paper snowflake stars to hang on the tree.
   a. Cut the paper into squares.
   b. Fold each square in half.
   c. Fold it again in the middle.
   d. Cut the folded paper as shown.
   e. Cut notches along the outside edges.
   f. Unfold the paper to see a snowflake star.
3. Make one snowflake star larger than the others.
4. Pull thread through each snowflake and tie a knot to fasten it.
5. Hang a snowflake star on the branch for each of the twelve days of Christmas. Hang the largest star on top of the tree for January 6, or Epiphany, the day when we celebrate the coming of the wise men.
6. Let the largest star remind you of the special star God put in the sky to lead the wise men to Jesus.

Other Ideas:
1. Cut stars from metallic paper.
2. Glue glitter on the stars.
3. Write Bible verses from the Christmas story or Old Testament prophesies of Christ on the stars.
4. Spray the branch with metallic paint or artificial snow. (This should be done by an adult.)

SS3847

God's Special Star

Starfish Ornament

Bible Story:
The wise men visit Jesus. Matthew 2:1-12

Materials:
Starfish
Acrylic paint
Brush
Glitter
Metallic thread
Scissors
Glue

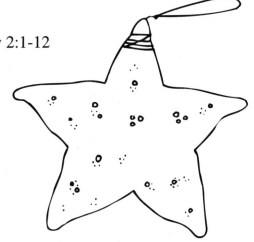

Directions:
1. Paint both sides of a starfish with acrylic paint.
2. Sprinkle glitter on the wet paint. Let it dry.
3. Cut a piece of metallic thread. Tie it around one of the starfish's legs. Fasten it with glue. Knot the thread a second time to make a hanger.
4. Hang the star on your Christmas tree. Let it remind you to seek Jesus this Christmas season as the wise men did so long ago.

Other Ideas:
Decorate the starfish with colored glue or different colors of glitter.

Shining Star Publications, Copyright © 1994

SS3847

I Become God's Child

Seashell Plaque

Bible Story:
Jesus' baptism. Matthew 3:13-17

Materials:
Block of wood
Scallop shell
Glue
Permanent markers
Sandpaper
Dark shoe polish
Rag
Eye hook

Directions:
1. The scallop shell has been used as a symbol of baptism. Make a scallop shell plaque as a reminder of your baptism.
2. Sand the wood block.
3. Screw the eye hook in the top of the block for a hanger.
4. Rub shoe polish on the wood block. Let it dry. Buff it with the rag.
5. Glue the scallop shell on the block.
6. Write your name and the date of your baptism on the plaque.
7. Talk about the meaning of baptism in your church.

Other Ideas:
1. Omit the baptismal date if you have not yet been baptized.
2. Write a Bible passage about baptism on the plaque. An appropriate passage might be the Great Commission passage, found in Matthew 28:19-20.

SS3847

Let Down Your Net

Leaf Collage

Bible Story:
  The great catch of fish. Luke 5:1-11

Materials:
  Styrofoam™ tray
  Blue construction paper
  Glue
  Scissors
  Fine-tipped markers
  Fish-shaped leaves (elm and
    apple leaves work well)
  Vegetable netting
  Large book
  Newspaper
  Cardboard roll

Directions:
  1. Gather fish-shaped leaves such as from an elm tree.
  2. Dry the leaves by placing them between sheets of newspaper and pressing them inside a large book for a week or two.
  3. Cut construction paper the size of the inside of the Styrofoam™ tray.
  4. Glue the leaves over the blue paper. Use markers to add fish details as well as other underwater life. Write "Let Down Your Nets" on the paper.
  5. Glue the paper inside the Styrofoam™ tray.
  6. Cut a piece of vegetable netting to drape and glue down inside the tray.
  7. Glue the cardboard tube to the back of the tray for a stand.
  8. Stand up your collage. Talk about ways you can "let down your nets" and tell others about Jesus.

Other Ideas:

  Glue the leaves to the paper, add details, and then place the paper between sheets of white paper and press in a large book to flatten the leaves. Write "Be Fishers of Men" on the sheet.

Blessed Are the Peacemakers

Pressed-Flower Bookmark

Bible Story:
The Beatitudes. Matthew 5:1-12

Materials:
Flowers and leaves
Newspaper
Large book
Clear adhesive plastic
Colored paper
Scissors
Calligraphy pen
Tweezers
Iron
Heavy white paper
Glue

Directions:
1. Dry flowers by placing them between pages of a newspaper inside a large book for three or four weeks.
2. Cut colored paper in a rectangle.
3. Use tweezers to move and arrange the flowers on the colored paper. (To avoid spots on the paper, use a small amount of glue.)
4. Use a calligraphy pen to write "Blessed Are the Peacemakers" on the paper.
5. Cover the bookmark with clear adhesive plastic.
6. Place the bookmark between two sheets of heavy white paper.
7. Have an adult iron the bookmark a few seconds on the cotton setting.
8. Let the bookmark remind you of your responsibility to be an instrument of God's peace in the world.

Other Ideas:
1. Make a pressed-flower picture containing other words from the Beatitudes.
2. Use colored poster board instead of colored paper.
3. Use other markers to draw a border along the sides of the bookmark.
4. Make pressed-flower pictures to illustrate other words of Scripture.
5. Cover both sides of the bookmark with clear adhesive plastic.

God Watches over Me

Feather Collage

Bible Story:

God watches over the birds. Matthew 6:25-26

Materials:

Paper plate
Markers
Feathers
Glue
Sunflower seeds (optional)
Hole punch

Directions:

1. Write "God Watches over Me" around the rim of the paper plate.
2. In the center of the plate, draw the outline of a bird.
3. Glue feathers to the bird shape.
4. Glue sunflower seeds around the bird's feet. (Optional)
5. Punch a hole at the top of the plate and hang it on your wall.
6. Talk about ways that God cares for the birds and how much more He cares for His children.

Other Ideas:

1. Instead of feathers, use seeds to fill in and outline the bird.
2. Create the bird on painted cardboard or a box lid instead of using a paper plate.

God Cares for You

Pressed-Flower Picture

Bible Story:

God cares for the flowers. Matthew 6:28-30

Materials:

Large book
Wildflowers
Tweezers
Styrofoam™ tray
Permanent markers
Plastic wrap
Yarn
Solid-colored fabric
Glue
Hole punch
Paper bag
Tape

Directions:

1. Go on a nature walk and pick wildflowers. Talk about the many different kinds of flowers God made.
2. Press the flowers between sheets of newspaper and place them inside a large book. Allow them to dry for three to four weeks.
3. Obtain a clean Styrofoam™ tray from a meat counter. Punch a hole in the center at the top. To make a hanger, string a piece of yarn through it and secure it with a knot.
4. Write "God Cares for You" around the rim of the tray.
5. Cut a piece of fabric the size of the inside of the tray. Glue it in place.
6. Cut yarn and glue it around the outside of the fabric and around the outside edge of the Styrofoam™ tray.
7. Use tweezers to place the dried flowers on the fabric. Very carefully glue them to the fabric.
8. Cut a piece of plastic wrap to go around the tray. Stretch it around the front of the tray and tape it to the back.
9. Hang your picture as a reminder of God's constant love for you.

Give Us This Day

Cornhusk Basket

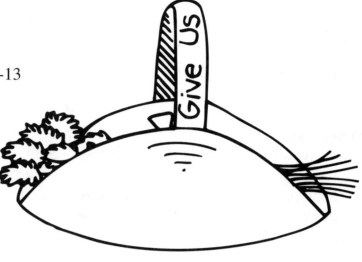

Bible Story:
The Lord's Prayer. Matthew 6:9-13

Materials:

Dried cornhusk
Water in a bowl
Scissors
Wheat stalks with grain
Glue
Paper clips
Ribbon
Markers

Directions:

1. Dry the cornhusk by spreading it out on a newspaper several days until it turns ivory in color.
2. Soak the dried cornhusk in water about ten minutes until it is pliable.
3. Fold the cornhusk. Cut a 3" x 2" oval through the two layers. Cut a 4" x 1" strip for the handle.

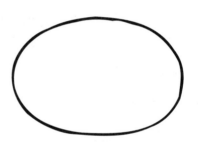

4. Glue the ovals together and clamp them together with paper clips. Fold up both sides of the basket.

5. Fold the strip lengthwise to make a 4" x ½" handle. Glue the handle to each side of the basket and fasten it with paper clips until it's dry.
6. Use a ribbon to tie a bow around several small stalks of wheat. Talk about how God's gift of wheat becomes the bread we eat each day.

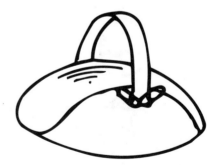

7. Write "Give Us This Day" on the basket handle. Let your basket remind you to thank God daily for His gift of daily bread.

Other Ideas:

1. Use the basket for small dried flowers or other objects that can illustrate other Bible lessons.
2. Tie a bow around the basket handle.

Twelve on a Mission

Rock Painting

Bible Story:

Jesus sends out the twelve.
Luke 9:1-6

Materials:

Twelve smooth stones
Acrylic paint
Small paintbrushes
Water

Directions:

1. Do this as a class project. Divide the disciples among the children. Each child or group may choose a disciple.
2. Paint the face of a disciple on each rock.
3. Use the rock heads to act out the message the disciples may have given to the people they met after Jesus' ascension.
4. Take your rock head home as a reminder that you, too, are called to spread the message of Jesus and His love.

Other Ideas:

1. Glue each rock on a block of wood which you have darkened with shoe polish.
2. Make a rock head to represent Jesus. Arrange the rocks around a box lid to illustrate the Last Supper.

Jesus Loves Me

Rock Brooch

Bible Story:

Jesus and the children. Luke 18:15-17

Materials:

Flat stone
Jewelry pin back
Hot glue gun
Acrylic paints
Pointed round paintbrush
Pencil

Directions:

1. Wash and dry the stone.
2. On the stone, lightly outline a pattern with a pencil. (Possible patterns are provided below.)
3. Paint the pattern on the stone.
4. Use a hot glue gun to fasten the jewelry pin back to the back of the rock brooch. (This should be done by an adult.)
5. Wear the brooch as a reminder that Jesus loves you just as He loved the children of His day.

Other Ideas:

1. Make several brooches to give to others as reminders that Jesus loves them.
2. Make brooches for Christmas or Easter gifts.
3. Cover the brooch with clear acrylic varnish after painting it, or cover it with acrylic first for a better surface on which to paint.
4. Fasten a safety pin to the back of the brooch with strong craft glue or a glue gun. (This should be done by an adult.)

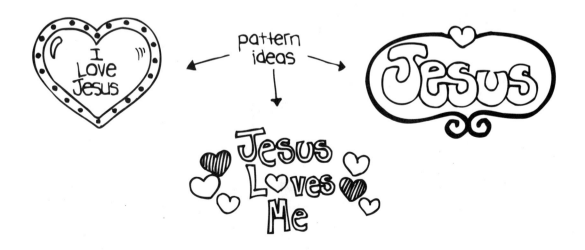

God Helps Me Move

Peanut Puppet

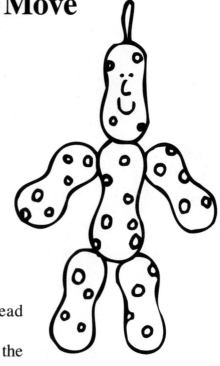

Bible Story:

Jesus heals a paralyzed man. Mark 2:1-12

Materials:

Six peanuts
Markers
Strong thread
Large needle
Scissors

Directions:

1. Thread the needle and knot it with the thread doubled.
2. Poke the needle through two peanuts to make the head and body of a man.
3. Connect two peanuts for legs and two peanuts for arms to the body.
4. Poke a loop at the top of the peanut for holding it up.
5. Use the markers to draw the man's face.
6. Tell the story of Jesus healing the paralyzed man. Move the puppet as you tell the story.

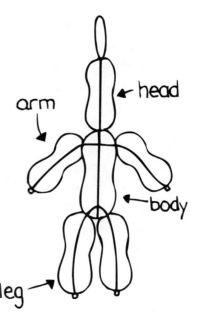

Other Ideas:

1. Cover the puppet with cloth for clothes.
2. Make peanut puppets of other people healed by Jesus.

Give Thanks

Dried-Bean Plaque

Bible Story:

Feeding the five thousand. John 6:1-14

Materials:

Large, round paper doily
Cardboard
Assorted dried beans
Empty cottage cheese container
Colored paper
Markers
Glue
Clear acrylic varnish
Bowl
Spoon
Ribbon (optional)
Scissors
Yarn

Directions:

1. Cut cardboard to fit about 1½" inside the paper doily.
2. Poke a hole in one end of the cardboard. Cut a piece of yarn and thread it through for a hanger.
3. Trace and cut out a construction paper circle from the top of an empty cottage cheese container. Write "Give Thanks to the Lord" on the circle or duplicate the pattern on page 46.
4. Glue the paper doily to the cardboard; glue the construction paper circle in the center.
5. Mix 1 to 1½ cups of beans together with acrylic varnish in a bowl to coat the beans. (Use more beans for a larger wreath.)
6. Place the cottage cheese container upside down over the cardboard circle. Spoon the coated beans on the cardboard circle around the container. Keep the beans on the cardboard, not on the paper doily on the outside. Remove the bowl.
7. Tie a ribbon into a bow and glue it to the bottom of the cardboard circle. (Optional)

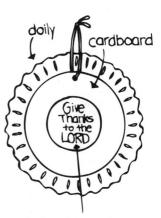

construction paper circle

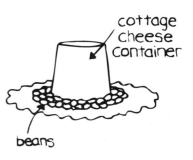

cottage cheese container

beans

8. Let it dry, and then hang the circle in your kitchen as a reminder to thank God for your food as Jesus did.

Other Ideas:
1. Write all of Psalm 107:1 in the center of the plaque.
2. Glue beans around the rim of a paper plate.
3. Use this project with other lessons emphasizing thanksgiving for God's gifts to us.
4. Use a variety of nature items for a Thanksgiving creation plaque.
5. Glue small pinecones around the plaque for a Christmas wreath.
6. Glue heads of wheat around the sides of the plaque and write "Give Us This Day Our Daily Bread" in the center.

Pattern:

SS3847

Zacchaeus, Come Down!

Pressed-Leaf Picture

Bible Story:
Jesus and Zacchaeus. Luke 19:1-10

Materials:
Leaves
Bark
Large book
Poster board
Markers or crayons
Glue
Gummed picture hanger
Newspaper

Directions:
1. Gather leaves.
2. Place the leaves between newspaper in a book for a week or two.
3. Glue bark to the poster board for a tree trunk.
4. Glue the leaves above the bark.
5. Draw two eyes in the tree to suggest Zacchaeus. Draw Jesus below.
6. Attach a gummed picture hanger to the back of the picture. Hang it as a reminder that Jesus wants all people to come to Him.

Other Ideas:
1. Cut a leaf into a shape to represent Jesus.
2. Make a backing from a piece of construction paper glued to a piece of cardboard, or paint the cardboard with tempera paint.
3. Use circle stickers for eyes. Draw pupils on the circles with a marker, or glue on movable eyes, available from craft stores.
4. Cover the picture with a sheet of plastic wrap.

Love One Another

Painted-Rock Paperweight

Bible Story:
The Good Samaritan. Luke 10:30-37

Materials:
Smooth, heart-shaped rock
Acrylic paint
Small paintbrush
Water

Directions:
1. Find a smooth, heart-shaped rock. Clean and dry it.
2. Paint "God Is Love" in the center of the rock.
3. Paint and repaint heart-shaped borders around the words until you reach the edge of the rock.
4. Use the rock as a paperweight. Let it remind you to show love to other people.

Other Ideas:
1. Omit the words and paint the heart outlines only.
2. Color the rock with permanent marker or tempera. Spray it with acrylic finish. (This should be done by an adult.)
3. Glue concentric felt hearts to a flat stone.
4. Paint rocks with enamel paint for a smooth, glossy finish, or paint them with acrylic finish before using acrylic paints.

From a Tiny Seed

Seeds in a Bottle

Bible Story:
Parable of the mustard seed.
Matthew 13:31-32

Materials:
Mustard seeds
Dried seeds
Empty baby food jar
Construction paper
Marker
Scissors
Glue

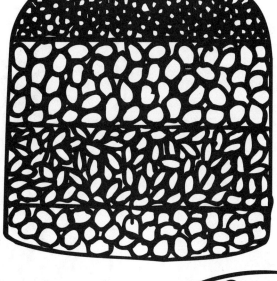

Directions:
1. Dry several different kinds of seeds on a cookie sheet. (Possible seeds to use include sunflower, watermelon, cantaloupe, and pumpkin.)
2. Layer seeds in the baby food jar. Separate them by cutting round paper circles to go between the different layers.
3. Add mustard seeds to the top layer. Talk about Jesus' parable about the mustard seed. Discuss how the plant that grows from it will be larger than the plant that grows from many other seeds. Think about small acts of kindness you can plant that will grow into big service for God and others.
4. Cut a paper circle to fit over the lid. Write "God's Kingdom Grows" on the circle. Glue the circle to the lid. Screw the lid tightly on the jar. If you wish, fasten the lid in place with glue.

Other Ideas:
1. Write words from the parable of the mustard seed on the lid.
2. Use a plastic or glass bottle.
3. Glue a mustard seed to the paper circle on top of the lid. Cover the circle with acrylic sealer. Fill the bottle with dried beans or other kinds of seeds.

Jesus' Little Lamb

Pinecone Figures

Bible Story:
Jesus is the Good Shepherd.
John 10:14

Materials:
Four pinecones
  (1 large and 3 small)
Six small sticks
  (about the same length)
One longer stick (about 2½
  times longer than the
  other sticks)
Wood glue
Modeling clay (optional)
Fine wire (optional)

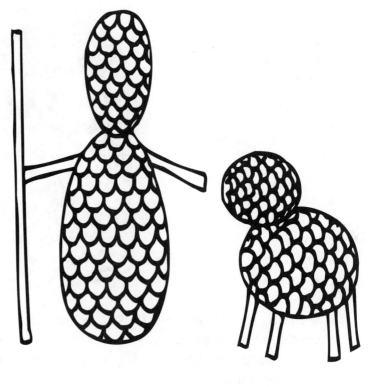

Directions:
1. Stand the large pinecone on its base. You may need to use modeling clay to make it stand.
2. Turn a smaller pinecone upside down; glue it on the top of the larger cone for the shepherd's head.
3. Glue two sticks on the large pinecone for arms.
4. Glue a stick on one arm for a staff.
5. Glue the smallest pinecone to the other pinecone for the lamb. (If necessary, tie the head down with fine wire.)
6. Glue on four sticks for legs.
7. Discuss how a good shepherd takes care of his lamb and how Jesus, your Good Shepherd, takes care of you.

Other Ideas:
1. Use construction paper, felt, or chenille stems to add details.
2. Use a pointed stick to connect the head of the sheep to its body.
3. Add color with acrylic paint.
4. Make several sheep to act out different sheep parables told by Jesus.
5. Glue the figures to a piece of cardboard. Add rocks and other nature objects.
6. Instead of twigs, use burnt matchsticks to make the arms and legs.
7. Use pinecones to make a variety of animals created by God.

Shining Star Publications, Copyright © 1994
SS3847

Alive in Christ

Shell Butterfly

Bible Story:
Jesus raised Lazarus from the dead. John 11:1-44

Materials:
Plastic lid
Felt or burlap
Two large shells
Two medium shells
Small shell
Oval shell
Glue
Colored glue
Scissors
Gummed picture hanger

Directions:
1. Cut felt or burlap to fit the plastic lid.
2. Glue the felt or burlap inside the lid.
3. Arrange the shells in a butterfly shape on the lid and glue them down. Then let them dry.
4. Attach a gummed picture hanger to the back of the lid.
5. Write "Alive in Christ" on the picture with colored glue. Talk about how a butterfly coming out of a cocoon can remind us of Jesus raising Lazarus to new life.
6. Attach the gummed hanger to the back of the lid. Hang up the plaque as a reminder that the risen Christ will one day raise you to new life with Him.

Other Ideas:
1. Use burlap or poster board instead of felt.
2. Instead of using felt or burlap, glue construction paper inside a Styrofoam™ tray. Write a Resurrection Bible passage around the tray's rim.
3. Make several butterflies and write "Alive in Christ" above them.

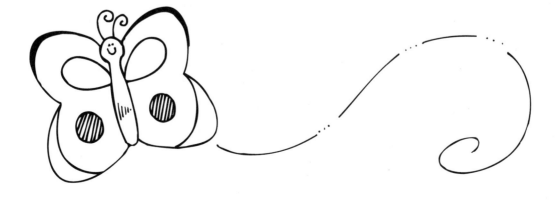

Hosanna to the King

Leaf Mobile

Bible Story:

Jesus rides into Jerusalem. John 12:12-15

Materials:

Leaves
Dowel stick
Construction paper
Needle
Strong thread
Glue
Waxed paper
Scissors
Newspaper
Large book
Hole punch

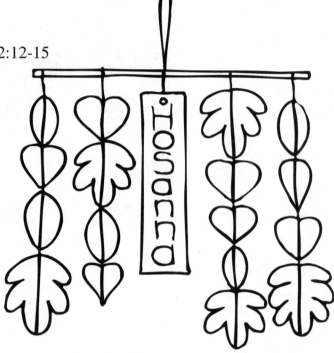

Directions:

1. When Jesus rode into Jerusalem, people waved palm leaves and threw them in His path. Use leaves found in your part of the country to make a mobile to praise Jesus. Place the leaves inside newspaper and press them in a large book for at least a week.
2. Lay the pressed leaves in four rows on top of a piece of waxed paper.
3. Cut a piece of thread about 6" longer than the row of leaves.
4. Spread glue down the middle of each leaf. Place the thread on the line of glue, leaving an extra 6" above the top leaf.
5. Cut a long strip of construction paper. Write "Hosanna" vertically on it. Punch a hole at the top and tie a 12" piece of thread through it.

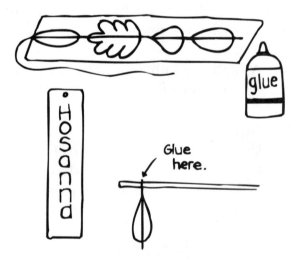

6. Tie the leaves to the stick, varying the length of each strand. Dot each knot with glue.
7. Tie the strip of construction paper 6" down from the center of the stick. Dot the knot with glue. Tie a loop at the top of the thread for hanging the mobile.
8. Hang your mobile to remind you to praise the Lord not just on Palm Sunday, but every day.

SS3847

Given for You

Seed Mosaic

Bible Story:
The Last Supper. Matthew 26:17-29

Materials:
Cardboard
Dried beans (red and white)
Clear acrylic sealer
Brush
Pencil
Scissors
Gummed picture hanger
Glue

Directions:
1. Duplicate and cut out the cup and bread pattern on page 54.
2. Trace the cup and bread pattern on cardboard and cut it out. Draw lines inside the pattern.
3. Glue red kidney beans all over the cup. Glue white navy beans all over the bread.
4. Attach a gummed picture hanger to the back of the pattern.
5. Discuss how your church celebrates the Lord's Supper. Hang your seed mosaic as a reminder of the first Lord's Supper.

Other Ideas:
1. Enlarge the pattern to fit on a round pizza cardboard. Use other colors of beans to fill in the background.
2. Use colored pebbles, egg shells, or rice instead of dried beans.
3. Use a third color of dried beans to outline the cup and add details.
4. Glue yellow corn on the cup shape instead of kidney beans.

Cup and Bread Pattern

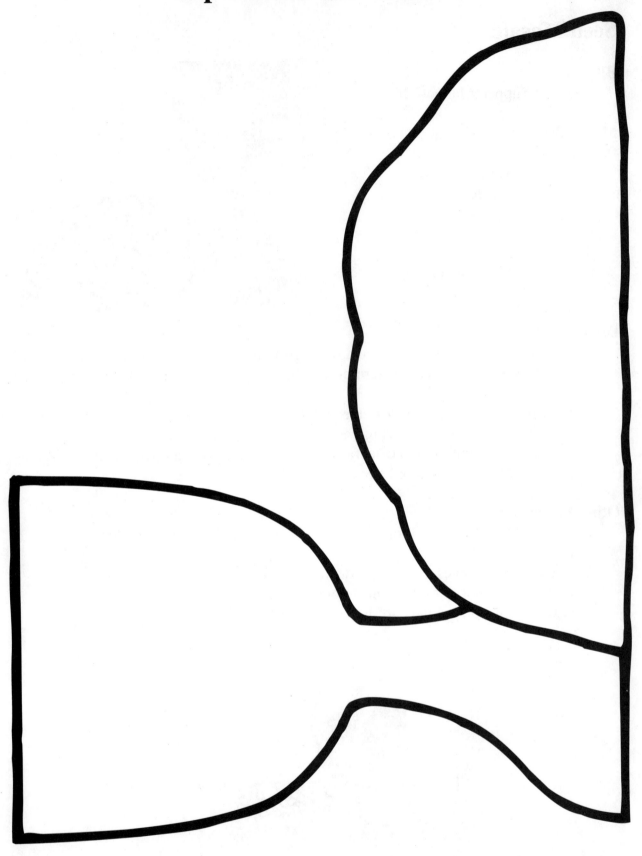

54

Thy Will Be Done

Shadow Box

Bible Story:
Jesus in Gethsemane.
Matthew 26:36-46

Materials:
Cardboard box
Tempera paint
Paintbrush and water
Branches
Glue
Black construction paper
Scissors
Pencil

Directions:
1. Paint the inside and outside of the cardboard box.
2. Stick branches inside the box, wedging them between the sides and top. Glue them in place, if necessary.
3. Duplicate the pattern of Jesus praying on page 56 on construction paper. Cut it out, fold the bottom tab back, and glue it to the bottom of the shadow box.

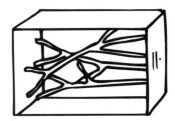

Other Ideas:
1. Glue a real rock on the bottom of the box and use chenille stems or clay to make a figure to represent Jesus.
2. Paint a picture of Jesus on bark or a wood scrap and glue it beside the rock.

tab

Shadow Box Pattern

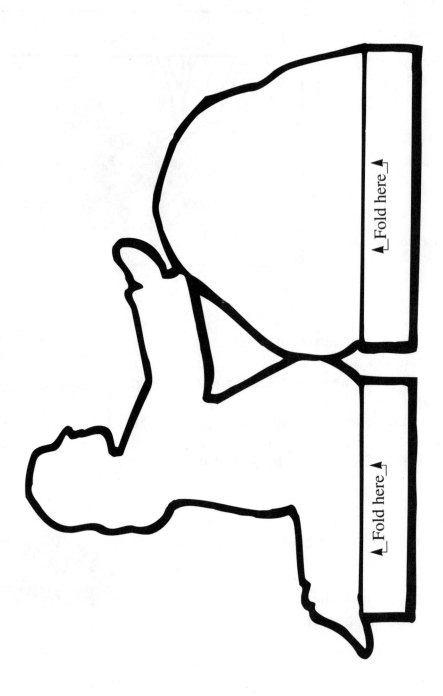

Fold here

Fold here

SS3847

He Died for You

Bark Cross

Bible Story:
Jesus' death on the cross. Luke 23:33-49

Materials:
Square piece of wood
Sandpaper
Bark
Glue
Eye hook
Clear acrylic sealer
Paintbrush
Water

Directions:
1. Sand the wood until it's smooth.
2. Attach the eye hook to the top of the board.
3. Glue pieces of bark on the wood in the shape of a cross.
4. Paint the cross and wood with clear acrylic sealer.
5. Hang the plaque in your home as a reminder that your sins have been forgiven because of Jesus' death.

Other Ideas:
1. Glue bark to a block of wood to make a stand-up cross.
2. Glue bark to a piece of cork.
3. Use bark for the hill of Calvary and twigs for the three crosses.

SS3847

The Empty Tomb

Rock Sculpture

Bible Story:
Jesus' resurrection. Luke 24:1-12

Materials:
Flat rock
Rounded rock
Flat, rounded rock
Glue
Acrylic paint
Small paintbrush
Nature objects (optional)

Directions:
1. Use the flat rock for the base; the rounded rock for the tomb; and the small, rounded, flat rock for the stone rolled away from the tomb.
2. Using heavy-duty glue, attach the tomb to the base and the flat rock to the tomb.
3. Use a small paintbrush to outline the door to the open tomb. Paint the inside yellow, with rays of light coming out from it. Above the door print the words of the angel, "He Has Risen!"
4. Glue moss, twigs, dry weeds, or other nature objects to the sides of the tomb. (Optional)
5. Let this rock sculpture be a daily reminder that Jesus rose from the grave, and He lives to hear and help you today.

Other Ideas:
1. Glue the tomb rock to cardboard or bark. Omit the stone for the open door; instead paint it on the side of the tomb rock.
2. Create a paperweight by painting an open tomb on a heavy, flat rock.
3. Cover your completed craft with clear acrylic sealer.
4. Paint the angels and women mentioned in the Bible story on the side of the tomb.
5. Paint Jesus beside the open tomb.

SS3847

Jesus Is Alive

Painted Eggs

Bible Story:
    Jesus walks with disciples on the road to Emmaus. Luke 24:13-35

Materials:
    Raw eggs
    Straight pin
    Permanent markers
    Acrylic sealer
    Pencil
    Toothpick

Directions:
1. Wash each egg. Using a straight pin, punch a hole in each end. Stick a toothpick in one end to break the yolk. Blow out the inside of the egg. Wash the egg again and let it dry.
2. Jesus told His disciples that the Scripture prophesied His birth and death. Make Scripture eggs to share the news of Jesus and His resurrection. Choose a symbol or word to put on the egg. You may want to duplicate, cut out, and trace one of the patterns on page 60 onto the egg. Add your own additional details.
3. Color the eggs with markers.
4. Paint the completed eggs with acrylic sealer.
5. Fill a basket with painted eggs for an Easter decoration or to give to someone else as a witness for Jesus.

Other Ideas:
1. Use watercolor markers; then spray the eggs with acrylic sealer.
2. Draw Christmas symbols on eggs to hang as tree decorations.
3. Hang witness eggs on a branch stuck into a jar of sand or pebbles.

Painted Egg Patterns

SS3847

Witness for the Lord

Pumpkin Seed Necklace

Bible Story:
The Great Commission.
Matthew 28:16-20

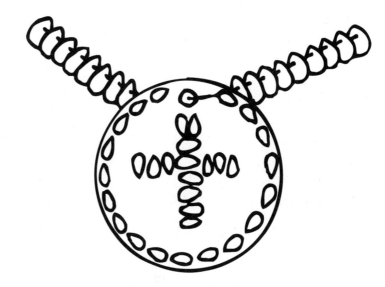

Materials:
Pumpkin seeds
Strong thread
Large needle
Plastic lid
Glue
Scissors
Hole punch

Directions:

1. Spread pumpkin seeds on a baking sheet and let them dry, or bake them in a 200°F oven until they're dry.
2. Glue the seeds on a plastic lid in the shape of a cross. Punch a hole at the top of the lid.

3. Cut double thread large enough to go over your head. Thread the needle and knot the ends.
4. String the pumpkin seeds by pushing the needle through the upper part of each seed. Then string the thread through the plastic lid.

Put needle through here...

5. Knot the thread and slip the necklace over your head. Wear it as a witness of your loving Savior.

Other Ideas:

1. String different kinds of seeds on the necklace.
2. Draw a cross on a large pumpkin seed. String the pumpkin seed and some watermelon seeds together for a necklace.
3. Glue a seed cross to a flat rock or a seashell.

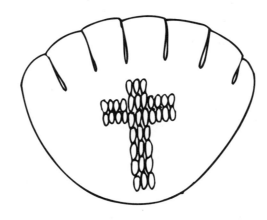

Shining Star Publications, Copyright © 1994

SS3847

Sailing for the Lord

Boat in a Bottle

Bible Story:
    Paul sails to spread the Gospel. Acts 13:4

Materials:
    Baby food jars
    Walnut shell half
    Oil-based clay
    Toothpick
    Fine-tipped markers
    Blue and white construction paper

Directions:
1. Trace a circle the size of the container's lid on construction paper. Cut it out and write "Spread the Good Word" on it. Glue it to the top of the lid.
2. Trace the bottom of the jar on construction paper. Cut it small enough to fit in the bottom of the jar.
3. Cut a strip of blue construction paper to fit around the jar. Cut waves in it and glue it around the inside of the jar. (Use the pattern below if needed.)
4. Cut a white sail for your "ship." (Use the pattern on this page if needed.) Draw a cross on it.
5. Poke the toothpick through the sail; then fasten it to the inside of the walnut shell with a piece of clay.
6. Glue the bottom of the walnut shell to the bottom of the jar.
7. Tighten the lid on the jar.
8. Display the boat as a reminder that you, too, are called by God to spread the Gospel.

sail pattern

Other Ideas:
1. Omit construction paper waves inside the jar; instead, place blue, oil-based clay inside it for waves. Stick the boat into the clay.
2. Write the words "Spread the Good Word" on the boat's sail.

God Sends the Seasons

Pressed-Leaf Sun Catcher

Bible Story:
Paul at Lystra. Acts 14:8-20

Materials:
Leaves
Large book
Waxed paper
Iron
Newspaper
Construction paper
Scissors
Glue
Hole punch
Yarn

Directions:

1. Place leaves between sheets of newspaper and press them for several days inside a large book.
2. Place the pressed leaves between two sheets of waxed paper. Put these between two sheets of newspaper and press with a hot iron. (This should be done by an adult.)
3. Cut two identical construction paper frames for your leaf sun catcher. (You may want to use the pattern on page 64.)
4. Glue a construction paper frame to either side of the waxed paper.
5. Trim the waxed paper to fit the frames.
6. Punch a hole at the top. Cut a piece of yarn and thread it through the hole for hanging.
7. Write "God Gives the Changing Seasons" around the construction paper frame. Talk about how Paul used a description of God's care in sending the seasons as a way of witnessing to the people of Lystra.

SS3847

8. Hang the sun catcher in your window as a witness to your belief in the God who "has shown kindness by giving us rain from heaven and crops in their seasons" (see Acts 14:17).

Other Ideas:
1. Adapt other words from Acts 14:17 for the sun catcher, such as "He Fills Our Hearts with Joy."
2. Iron flowers and weeds inside waxed paper to make a sun catcher emphasizing God's care for the flowers and for us.

Pattern: